CHRISTMAS
WINDOW ART

by Barbara Kane

KLUTZ®

The squeeze bottles on the front of this book are filled with a special squirt-on paint that dries in 24 hours to make a tough film that you can peel off and stick to glass windows and mirrors. Get adult help to cut the case of bottles and the two plastic sleeves from the book before you begin.

WHAT IS WINDOW ART?

1.

PICK A DESIGN and slip one of the plastic sleeves over that page in the book.

2.

TRACE the lines of the design with the black outline paint. The black makes a wall to hold the colors. (If you let the black dry for a while first, it makes the next step easier.)

3.

FILL IN the spaces with your choice of colors. Be generous, but don't let the color overflow.

4.

LET THE PIECE DRY for at least 24 hours. At this time tomorrow, check to see if it's dry to the touch and ready for peeling.

5.

PEEL YOUR DESIGN OFF the plastic and stick it to a window. **WOW!**

It's as easy as squirting toothpaste on a brush!

How do I use the designs in this book?

TRACE ┈┈┈┈┈> SQUIRT ┈┈┈┈┈> PEEL ┈┈┈┈┈> STICK!

WINDOW ART WORKS BEST AT T-SHIRT TEMPERATURES

This is the range where you are comfortable in jeans and a T-shirt.

THE IMPORTANCE OF PLASTIC.

You have to trace and squirt your designs onto the right kind of plastic (never onto paper!) or you won't be able to peel them off. Use the plastic sleeves from this book – get adult help to cut them out – or use zipper-style plastic bags or plastic page protectors. If you have used the right kind of plastic, and have let the colors dry thoroughly, but are having trouble peeling off your design, try putting the piece in the refrigerator for a few minutes before peeling.

gets soft and sticky

stays bendable and tacky

80°F

gets stiff and brittle

50°F

3

DON'T LET A FINISHED PIECE FOLD BACK ON ITSELF.

This is something to watch out for while peeling a piece off the plastic. If two areas touch, they could stick together permanently. If you put a piece that's just gotten stuck in the refrigerator for a minute or two, you might be able to coax the layers apart.

The **black outline** paint is thicker than the **FILL COLORS**, which are thin and flowing. The fill colors don't work well for outlining and the black is good for filling in only very small spaces.

PLASTICS CAUTION: Because Window Art Colors are plastic, even a finished piece can become permanently bonded to other plastic surfaces, including some paints and wood finishes. Put Window Art pieces on glass windows, mirrors and glassware only.

4

CLOTHING CAUTION: The colors tend to stain clothes, rugs, upholstery, etc., especially if the colors dry before washing. Our advice? Don't work in the living room, and wear something that could use a little decoration, anyway.

Cuffs on long sleeves are likely targets for wet paint. So, roll up those sleeves!

LOOK! You can make this Santa tumble across your windows like we did… just make several of the same piece and arrange them like this.

MESS-UPS HAPPEN. If some of the window paint gets onto a part of your piece where it just wasn't supposed to be, you can usually wipe it away before it dries by using a cotton swab.

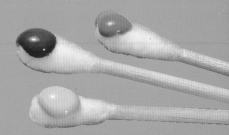

You can dress up your Window Art by sprinkling on a little glitter before the colors dry. Look for fine, transparent glitter that will let the light through.

You can store window art for next year in zipper bags or page protectors. (The surface might change a little, but they will still be beautiful!) Don't layer your pieces with paper or plastic wrap because they will stick badly.

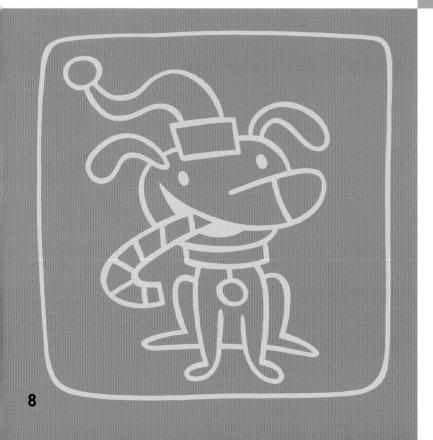

8

YOUNGER KIDS? We can do window art, too. Just do the black outlining for us and let it dry before we fill in the colors.

Yellow paint squirting slowly? That's normal for a window color that contains glitter. It takes a little longer and a bit more squeezing to coax it out of the bottle.

9

HERE'S A HINT: This artist uses black lines that cross over into the colored spaces. If you can wait, let the lines dry before you fill in the color.

You can make a **colorful garland** like we did, making ● *tiny "beads"* by adding dots of Window Art color directly on the window after you've put the bigger decorations in place. ● Keep these colored beads small - *no bigger than we've shown here* ● - so the paint doesn't run down the glass.

REMEMBER:
ONLY THE BLACK PAINT
WILL WORK TO MAKE
THE OUTLINES.

TO:

YOU CAN MAKE A BIG TREE OUT OF THESE SMALLER ONES. Make ten individual trees and arrange them as we've shown here!

19

BLACK ICICLES??
We like the look of the icicles without black outlines. Just cover each icicle shape with a layer of white paint.

IMPORTANT SNOWFLAKE TIP

Because it's so hard to peel delicate snowflakes off the plastic without ruining them, we like to make them directly on the window. Have a helper stand outside and hold the book up against the window while you trace the pattern from the inside. Go easy with the paint so it won't drip.

23

Because of their shapes, be extra careful when you peel these critters off the plastic.

24

THE PEA RULE:

If you want to design your own Window Art template, use a medium-tip marker and make sure that all of your spaces are at least as large as a pea... like these.

1/4"

PATTERN TURN-AROUND TRICK

With the help of a window and a photocopier, we made a mirror image of the angel corner design so that we could put one in each corner of the window.

1. First, photocopy the design onto blank white paper.

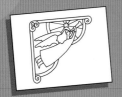

2. Turn the paper over and tape it onto any handy window with the picture facing outside. The light coming through the window (you can only do this when it's light out) will make the design show through the paper.

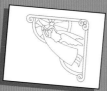

3. Trace over all the lines with a pencil or black marker. This will give you a reverse image of the design in the book.

4. Make one piece from the design in the book, the other from your tracing.

A PERFECT MATCH!

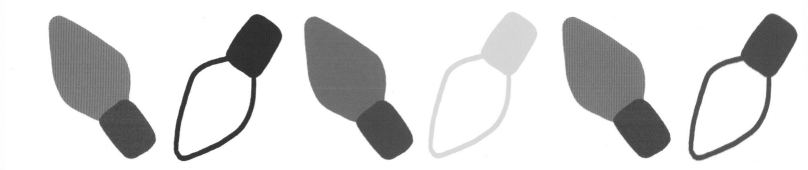

Christmas Lights

To make a string of lights, draw a wire with black paint directly on the window.

Yours might be the only window on the block to have Christmas lights that:

- look better from inside the house
- are only visible during the daytime
- don't use any electricity at all!

We think this is a design that looks good without black outlining around the colored glass part of each light.

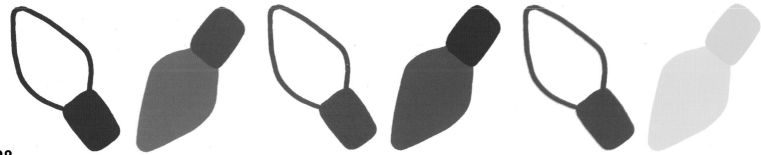

32

This one only looks complicated...use this coloring guide to help you make a masterpiece!

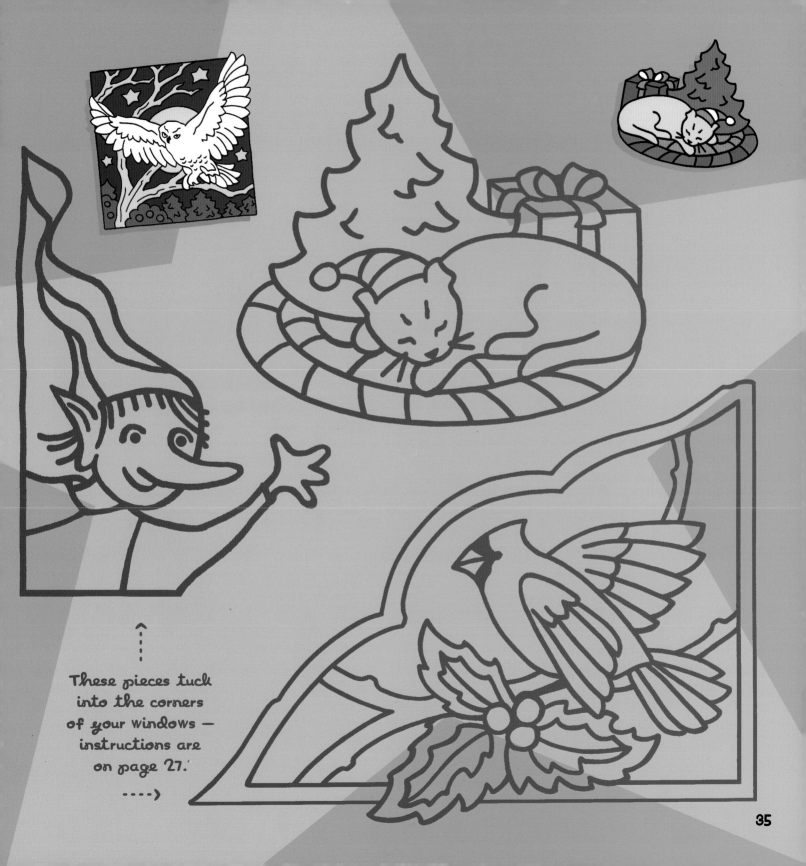

These pieces tuck
into the corners
of your windows —
instructions are
on page 27.

----->

SANTA'S HELPERS

Here are the real people who did their part to create this book:

BOOK DESIGN: Maria Seamans

COVER DESIGN & ART DIRECTION: Elizabeth Buchanan

ILLUSTRATORS: Linda Ann Buonocore, Dorota Lagida, Mary Anne Lloyd, Gary Morgan, Bud Peen, Mary Thelen, Erica Thurston, Alice Tucker, Martha Vercoutere, Stacie Wong

JOLLY OL' ELF: John Cassidy

PHOTOGRAPHY: Peter Fox, Tom Upton

BACKGROUND PHOTOGRAPHS: COVER: © Frank Siteman/Index Stock Imagery/PictureQuest. INSIDE FRONT COVER: Envelopes © 1998-2001 EyeWire, Inc. All rights reserved. TITLE PAGE: Snowy Tree, H. Wiesenhofer/ PhotoLink.

PAINT ELF: Kelly Shaffer

THE PIXELATOR: David Barker

PHOTO SAMPLES: Rachelle Adams, Elizabeth Buchanan, Linda Ann Buonocore, Jenny Hsin, Elizabeth Kobsell, Mollie Malone, Sharon Palmer, Megan

Smith, Alice Tucker, and Ruth Wilson

MODEL WRANGLING: Susan Fox

MODELS: Louise Barnett, Samantha Cuerington, Lori Cuerington, James Harrison, Kelsey Feeley, Jenner Fox, Kaela Fox, Keely Haverstock, Colin Kelly, Sarah Nishimoto, Steven Nishimoto, Trevor Remmel, Anna Rizza, Michael Starr, Chantal Taylor, Jamie Tipton, Melissa Tipton, Domino the dog

KEEPING THE WINDOW ART FLOWING: Megan Smith

SPECIAL THANKS: Taylor Seamans

Can't Stop Creating Window Art?

Some people, we've noticed, really like doing Window Art. If you need a replacement set of Window Colors, you can order them from our mail order catalog. For those of you who have been canceling out on birthday parties to stay home and work on your Window Art projects, we also offer the 18-bottle Window Art Fanatic Set, which includes very cool colors like sparkle pink and crystal clear.

To get the catalog, send us the postcard below or visit us at KLUTZ.COM.

Klutz Catalog!

You can order the entire library of 100% Klutz certified books, replacement window colors, and a diverse collection of other things we happen to like from The Klutz Catalog. It is, in all modesty, unlike any other catalog — and it's yours for the asking.

Who are you?

Name: _____ Age: _____ ❑ Too high to count ◯ Boy ◯ Girl

Address: _____

City: _____ State: _____ Zip: _____

My Bright Ideas!

Tell us what you think of this book: _____

_____

What would you like us to write a book about? _____

_____

❑ Check this box if you want us to send you The Klutz Catalog.

If you're a grown-up who'd like to hear about new Klutz stuff, give us your e-mail address and we'll stay in touch.

E-mail address: _____

First Class
Postage
Here

KLUTZ®
455 Portage Avenue
Palo Alto, CA 94306